Ideas for success, wealth and happiness

Great Lessons from Great Minds

By Jim Yih

Think Box Consulting

Cover Design: Jim Yih

Great Quotes from Great Minds
Copyright © 2011 Think Box Consulting Inc and Jim Yih

For information address: Think Box, 7614-119 Street, Edmonton, Alberta Canada. T6G 1W3
www.thinklots.com

FIRST EDITION

Printed in Canada

100% to Charity

For the past 20 years, my professional passion has been helping people make better decisions with money. My career has been sincerely gratifying because of all the people that have benefited from my advice, articles, education and books.

In 2007, I was really fortunate to have sold my wonderful client practice to pursue more opportunities to put unique financial education programs into the workplace as opposed to product oriented solutions.

At that time we started the YIH CHARITABLE GIVING FUND through the Edmonton Community Foundation (ECF). I am very proud that 100% of profits from this book will be donated to our giving fund through the ECF.

Your support will help support charities in our community that help children because they represent our future.

Thank you!
Jim

Dedication

This book is dedicated to 5 special people that have changed my life in more ways than I will ever know: Robbie, Connor, Jason, Brandon and my darling Elizabeth. You inspire me! You complete me! You give me purpose!

I love you guys!

Contents

Introduction

All of my inspiration comes from other people. Sometimes it's people I know like my mentors, associates, and clients. Inspiration also comes from friends and especially my family. Sometimes my inspiration even comes from people I have never met and the brilliant things they say.

I love quotes. I always have. In this book, I want to share with you some of my favorite quotes that I have collected over the years and have meaning in my life. These quotes continue to inspire me to better myself and inspire those around me.

Whenever I need a little inspiration, motivation or pick me up, I take 15 to 20 minutes to read some of these quotes and reflect on what I am doing.

My real hope and inspiration for the book

Inspiration is always the catalyst for accomplishment. I'm proud of my successes in life and one of my biggest accomplishments is becoming a husband and a dad. My family has really changed my life.

My confession is I really wrote this book for my kids because more than anything I want my kids to know that their life is not to be taken for granted. I want my kids to know what it took to create the life they currently have. If I can give them this understanding, then that will be one of the best gifts I can give them.

I have put together this little book of ideas and quotes in hopes that anyone but especially my kids might find thoughts to achieve more success, wealth and happiness in life.

I hope this book not only becomes inspiration for my kids but also inspiration for you as well. I hope you enjoy!

Jim

p.s Here's what I love most about quotes:

They may tell you things you already know but they may also tell you something you know but forgot was important.

Quotes on
SUCCESS

Success for me is not a destination but a journey of milestones and achievements. If I were to create the perfect recipe for success, it would have a lot of ingredients like passion, hard work, luck, action, belief, dreams, conviction, focus, consideration, experience, discipline, consistency, and ethics.

When I do my life planning, I like to break my life into a few big categories or areas. I call these areas my big rocks: personal achievement, health, relationships, wealth, business, faith and community. Big or small, I try to find successes in different aspects of my life. Success is just taking one step at a time towards any destination one desires.

These great quotes on success really sum up my beliefs and values on this important topic.

"Success is not a secret - it never has been. There are only a few really good ideas and not one of them is a secret."
Larry Winget

"If you don't know what you want, you won't know when you've gotten it."

"Success isn't the key to happiness. Happiness is the key to success."

"If you love what you're doing, you'll be successful."
Albert Schweitzer

"Quality is never an accident; It is the result of intelligent efforts."
John Ruskin

"Knowing is not enough...we must apply;
Willing is not enough...we must do."
Goethe

"Whether you think you can or can't,
you're right."
Henry Ford

"There is no way to know before
experiencing."
Dr. Robert Anthony

"Some men see things as they are and ask
why. Others dream things that never were
and ask why not."
George Bernard Shaw

"I don't know the key to success, but the key
to failure is to try to please everyone."
Bill Cosby

"God gave people a mouth that closes and ears that don't, which should tell us something."

"God gave us two ears and one mouth. Use them in proportion."
My Mom
(when she wanted me to listen)

"There are times when silence has the loudest voice."
Leroy Brownlow

"Experience is a hard teacher because she gives the test first, the lesson afterwards."
Vernon Sunders Law

"He who begins many things finishes but a few."

"Diligence is the mother of good luck."
Ben Franklin

"Every waking moment is another chance to turn things around and change your life."
From the movie Vanilla Sky

"There are half a dozen things in anything you do that makes 80% of the difference. Figure out those half a dozen things and you can't help but find success."
Jim Rohn

"Some say the key to success is to work smarter, NOT harder. I think the key is to work smarter AND harder."
Jim Yih

"It's funny how the harder you work, the luckier you get."

"Success is doing ordinary things
extraordinarily well."
Jim Rohn

"Success is not to be pursued; it is to be
attracted by the person you become."
Jim Rohn

"Success is nothing more than a few simple
disciplines, practiced every day."
Jim Rohn

"Spend the remaining hours of your life only
on those activities that will yield you the
highest return on investment."
Robin Sharma

"The smallest of actions is always better than
the noblest of intentions."
Robin Sharma

"Work does not feel like work if you love the work you are doing."

"It may be those that DO the most are also those that DREAM the most."
Stephen Leacock

"Successful people do not do what is convenient. They do what's right."
Robin Sharma

"Success is neither magical nor mysterious. Success is the natural consequence of consistently applying the basic fundamentals."
Jim Rohn

"Success is not a destination; it's a journey."
Zig Ziglar

"You will succeed the minute you get rid of all the reasons and obstacles you can't."
Lou Holtz

"Live the life you have designed by achieving your definition of success."

"Winners never quit!
Quitters never win!"

"Success is designed. There is a formula to success. The key is to find it and then practice it every day of your life."

notes

notes

notes

Quotes on
WEALTH

Back in 1991, I graduated from the University of Alberta with a Bachelor of Commerce degree. It was tough times back then and jobs were pretty scarce.

Some of my friends knew exactly what they wanted to do for their professional career but I didn't! As a result, I applied for anything and everything.

After sending out what seemed like hundreds of resumes and only a handful of interviews, I was offered two jobs; One in commercial realty and the other with a big insurance company as an investment specialist. I took the investment job with the insurance company because it paid $28,800 per year plus benefits while the commercial realty position paid $16,000 per year with no benefits. It was not a tough decision.

Little did I know that would be the catalyst to my professional passion of helping people make better decisions about wealth, money, investing, retirement and personal finance.

"Money can't buy you happiness but it does bring you a more pleasant form of misery."

"Money was never a big motivation for me, except as a way to keep score. The real excitement is playing the game."
Donald Trump

"The richest person is not the one who has the most, but the one who needs the least."

"A wise man should have money in his head, but not in his heart."
Jonathan Swift

"Money is better than poverty, if only for financial reasons."
Woody Allen

"Every morning I get up and look through the Forbes list of the richest people in America. If I'm not there, I go to work."
Robert Orben

"Once you begin taking care of your money, I can promise that your money in turn will take care of you."
Suze Orman

"There are two things needed in these days: first for rich men to find out how poor men live and second for poor men to know how rich men work."
E. Atkinson

"The best things in life are free, but the next best things are expensive."
Gail Val Oxlade

"The wealthiest people in the world aren't those with the most stuff. They are the ones who manage their lifestyle the best."
Diane McCurdy

"Bank accounts are like toothpaste: easy to take out but hard to put back in."
Robert Ackerstrom

"Money goes where it is appreciated and stays where it is treated best."

"Spending make us feel rich but the only way to become rich is to watch your spending so you can save money."

"Debt has changed the way we think about wealth. We have moved from <u>delayed gratification</u> to <u>delayed consequence</u>."

"Today our priorities have shifted. Instead of pursuing <u>actual wealth</u>, we now spend more time on pursuing the <u>perception of wealth</u>."

"You have the same rights and opportunities as everyone else to be as wealthy as you want."
Richard Templar

"I've been rich and I've been poor. Believe me, rich is better."
Sophie Tucker

"Having more wealth may not change your habits. In fact, more money might just accentuate the habits you already have."

"Wealth is about **more**
Prosperity is about **enough**."
Francis D'Andrade

"Rich people focus on what they want, while poor people focus on what they don't want."
T Harv Ecker

"If you want more wealth, you need to know the difference between an asset and a liability . . . and buy more assets."
Robert Kiyasaki

"If you see money as the solution, you will find it becomes the problem."
Richard Templar

"In my experience, getting rich takes focus, courage, knowledge, expertise, 100 percent of your effort, a never-give-up attitude and a rich mind-set.
T Harv Ecker

"If you are broke, just remember . . .
You're broke because you want to be."
Larry Winget

"Wealth is not the same as income. If you make a good income but spend it all, you are not getting any wealthier. Wealth is what you accumulate, not what you spend."
From the Millionaire Next Door

"Wealth is achievable. It is built one step at a time by paying yourself first."

"Most people spend first and save what little they have left over. The secret to wealth is to always pay yourself first before anyone else. You are worth it!"

notes

notes

Quotes on
HAPPINESS

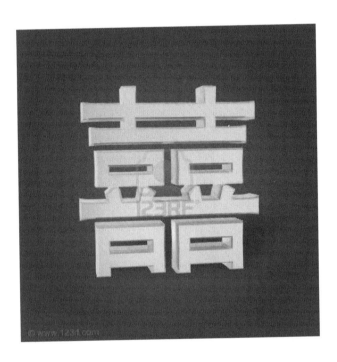

My wife Liz is genuinely the happiest person I know. She should be . . . she has me!

In all seriousness, I think one of the best ways to be happy is to simply be around happy people. Happiness is contagious. One of the best ways to learn how to be happy is to watch happy people and learn from their actions. Here's what Liz has taught me about happiness:

- Treat others as you want them to treat you
- Always help others without expecting anything back
- Appreciate what you have and take time to know that your glass is more full than you think.
- Have compassion and listen to others
- Smile, then laugh. Laugh, then smile. It's all contagious
- Take time for yourself to do what you love to do (like run a half marathon).
- Surround yourself with people that make you happy.

Sometimes we think to be happy, we need to be selfish but what Liz has taught me is that happiness comes from helping others become happy first. It's all about people, relationships and sharing.

Happiness comes in appreciating what you have instead of always trying to get more, have more and do more.

"The happiest people don't <u>have</u> the best of everything. They just <u>make</u> the best of everything!"

"Yesterday is dead, tomorrow hasn't arrived yet. I have just one day, today, and I'm going to be happy in it."
Groucho Marx

"It's not about getting what you want. It's about wanting what you got."
Sheryl Crow

"Each morning when I open my eyes I say to myself: I have the power to make me happy or unhappy. I can choose which it shall be. "
Groucho Marx

If you want others to be happy, practice compassion. If you want to be happy, practice compassion.
Dalai Lama

"Food makes people happy. Food makes me happy. You can eat anything you want as long as it is in moderation."
Liz Yih

"If you want to be happy, set a goal that commands your thoughts, liberates your energy, and inspires your hopes."
Andrew Carnegie

"Thousands of candles can be lighted from a single candle, and the life of the candle will not be shortened. Happiness never decreases by being shared."
Buddha

"Most people are about as happy as they make up their minds to be."
Abraham Lincoln

"People say that money is not the key to happiness, but I always figured if you have enough money, you can have a key made."
Joan Rivers

"Happiness is never stopping to think if you are or aren't."

"Happiness comes from surrounding yourself with happy people."

"Happiness is not something ready made. It comes from your own actions."
Dalai Lama

"The shortest distance between two points is the most enjoyable one."

"Happiness is when what you <u>think</u>, what you <u>say</u> and what you <u>do</u> are all in harmony."
Ghandi

"Happiness is not an accident.
Nor is it something you wish for.
Happiness is something you design."
Jim Rohn

"Happiness comes when you believe and love what you are doing."
Brian Tracy

"You already possess all you need to be genuinely happy."
Sarah Ban Breathnach

notes

notes

notes

Quotes on
RETIREMENT

Retirement has come a long way. There was a time, when retirement was really a short window in our lives where we were considered old and maybe even useless. This happened at a time when it was mandatory to retire at the age of 65 and we statistically lived till 70.

Today, retirement is very different. Today, we see a lot of retirees who are busier in retirement than before they retired. The retiree today is capable of so much more simply because the retiree today is younger physically, mentally and spiritually. Retirement today can last 15, 20, 30 years or more.

In my retirement workshops, I share a lot of information but I think the most important message I preach is there is no universal definition of what retirement means anymore. Retirement can be anything you want it to be. The secret is to figure out what you want it to be. Hopefully some of these quotes can help you figure out what you want it to be.

"If retirement is a time to write a new chapter in your life, start writing the chapter now!"

"If you enjoy what you do, you will never work a day in your life."
Aristotle

"The secret to a successful retirement is to find your retirement sweet spot. The sweet spot is where your *passions*, *what you do best*, and *what people will pay you to do* overlap."
Jim Collins

"A car's windshield is large and the rearview mirror is small because our PAST is not as important as our FUTURE.
Look ahead and move on."

"Retirement for some people is the dream for the perfect life they never had while they were working. For others retirement may not be 'the dream' but rather an extension of the life you are already living."
Jim Yih

"Happy people before retirement are generally happy people in retirement. Grumpy people before retirement are generally grumpy people in retirement. Work on being happy before you retire."
Jim Yih

"The trouble with retirement is that you never get a day off."
Abe Lemons

"When a man retires, his wife gets twice the husband but only half the income."

"Retirement is the ugliest word in the English language."
Ernest Hemingway

"A retired husband is often a wife's full-time job."

"Retired is being twice <u>tired</u>:
First <u>tired</u> of working,
Then <u>tired</u> of not."

"The last thing you want in retirement is to become bored because boredom leads to depression and depression leads to taking little pills and then you ultimately die grumpy."
Jim Yih

"The challenge of retirement is how to spend time without spending money."

"Retirement is wonderful. It's doing nothing without worrying about getting caught at it."
Gene Perret

"Why wait till retirement to retire? Why not make today the best years of your life?"
Jim Yih

"Everyone retires <u>from</u> something. The key to success is to retire <u>to</u> something."

"The best time to retire is when you are ready. You'll know you are ready when you are ready. Readiness is more of a lifestyle issue than a money issue."

"Retirement might be the most important vacation in your life. Plan your retirement like you plan your vacations."

"The key to success is to retire from work without retiring from your life."

"Retirement is a time to be selfish and you can tell your spouse I said so! . . . Because I will tell your spouse the same thing."
Jim Yih

"A happy and successful retirement comes from being happy and successful before you retire."

"Retirement is less about saving and more about spending."
Rein Selles

"When you retire,
think and act as if you were still working.
When you are still working,
think and act as if you were already retired."

"If all your retirement plans center around
the 4 weeks you are going to travel, what are
you going to do the other 48 weeks of the
year?"

"Every day is a chance to start living a new
life. You don't need retirement to do that."

"Retirement should simply be your preferred
lifestyle. Why would you retire if you cannot
see your life in retirement as better than the
life you are currently living."
Rein Selles

"Retirement is about figuring out what you are going to do <u>most</u> of the time, not <u>some</u> of the time!"

"Most retirement planning is done in the coffee room where people who know nothing teach other people what to do."

"Retirement planning is the harmonization of two critical issues: money issues and lifestyle issues. The more these 2 issues overlap, the more successful retirement will be."

notes

notes

notes

Quotes on
INVESTING

Investing is another one of those things that has become ridiculously confusing and complex. Google the word 'investing' and you will find 139,000,000 results in 0.11 seconds. There is no shortage of information on the topic.

As complex as it can be, I believe investing does not need to be so complicated. In fact, I think investing is not rocket science.

I've done a lot of research on investing. It started back in 1997 when I started doing research to try to develop a 'filter' for selecting top quality mutual funds. Eventually that research became the content for my best selling book Mutual Fundamentals.

All of my research has lead me to believe that the biggest determinant of success or failure lies in you and your ability to overcome emotion and psychology. Investing is more of a psychological game than a technical game.

"We simply attempt to be fearful when others are greedy and to be greedy only when others are fearful."
Warren Buffett

"In this business if you're good, you're right six times out of ten. You're never going to be right nine times out of ten."
Peter Lynch

"Many of the biggest and most far-reaching investments we make in our lives are investments that have little or nothing to do with money."
Daniel Quinn

"Nobody is born a great investor. It takes hard work, discipline and determination."
Thomas White Jr.

"Investing is an inexact science. It is better to be approximately right than precisely wrong."
George Hartman

"There are two rules to investing:
Rule #1 - Never Ever Lose Money
Rule #2 - Never Ever Forget Rule #1"
My mother

"Investors always do the wrong things at the wrong time. They buy when they should sell and they sell when they should buy."
Nick Murray

"Investing without research is like playing stud poker without looking at the cards."
Peter Lynch

"If you buy CRAP and hold CRAP, you will always have the one thing that stinks – CRAP!"
Jim Yih

"There is only one way to avoid crap – Research. Do you do research?"

"There is no such thing as perfection when it comes to investing. Success comes from increasing your probability of being right more often than wrong and making money more often than losing money."

"To invest successfully over a lifetime does not require stratospheric I.Q., unusual business insight or inside information. What is needed is a sound intellectual framework for making decisions and the ability to keep emotions from corroding that framework."
Warren Buffet

"The true secret of success in the investment and speculative world is not so much which good securities to buy, but rather which investments to avoid."
Morton Shulman

"In the investment game, risk and return are inseparable."
Donald Kurtz

"Everyone has the brain power to make money in stocks. Not everyone has the stomach."
Peter Lynch

"Your ultimate success or failure will depend on your ability to ignore the worries of the world long enough to allow your investments to succeed. It isn't the head but the stomach that determines the fate of the stock-picker."
Peter Lynch

"There are two times in a man's life when he should not speculate: when he can't afford to and when he can."
Mark Twain

"One of the safest times to invest is when the news is awful and markets are depressed: the time of deepest gloom"
John Train

"History has shown that the contrarian attitude has always paid off over time. We are not about to defy history."
Michael Lee Chin

"There is a big difference between investing FOR retirement and investing IN retirement."
Jim Yih

The key to making money in stocks is not to get scared out of them.
Peter Lynch

"October is one of the most dangerous months to speculate in stocks.
The others are January, February, March, April, May, June, July, August, September, November and December."
Mark Twain

"Never invest in any idea you can't illustrate with a crayon."
Peter Lynch

"The safe way to double your money is to fold it over once and put it in your pocket."

"Good Research Leads to Good Decisions."
Jim Yih

"This time is different" are among the most costly four words in history."
Sir John Templeton

"The difference between success and failure does not lie in studying <u>investment</u> behavior as much as it lies in understanding <u>investor</u> behavior."

"Buy low, sell high is a sure bet to making money. Unfortunately it is not the predominate strategy preached by the investment industry. Instead it's buy and hold."
Jim Yih

"Buy and hold ignores one of the key decisions to making money – the sell decision."
Jim Yih

"Buy and hold does not mean ignore."

"Nobody cares about your money more than you care about your money. If you don't care, who will?"
Jim Yih

"It is human nature to feel the pain of loss twice as much as the joy of gain."

"Trying to predict the future of the stock market, the economy or an investment is a waste of good energy. It's better to focus your energy on things that you can control like managing cashflow and paying down debts."

notes

notes

Quotes on
PLANNING

Some people say I am so lucky to have what I have. I don't think it has much to do with luck. My success and accomplishments are planned. Some people are good at winging it. Not me.

I'm a little biased but I think if people just take time out of their busy lives to do some planning to recognize what is important, everyone will be 'luckier'.

No matter how busy I am, I always take time to plan my future. I spend more time on planning than I do on execution and follow up. I like to dream and I like to plan but as much as I like both of these things, the ultimate key is to execute the plan.

Success comes from looking in the to future to make that future as predictable as possible.

The lottery is an example of random luck. I much prefer planned luck. You should give it a try! You might be surprised at the results.

"If you don't know where you are going,
any road will do."
Confucius

"Every road will take you 'somewhere'
but is that 'somewhere' really where you
want to go?"

"The best way to predict the future is to
create it."

"There is nothing new in the world except the
history you do not know."
Harry S Truman

"History never repeats itself, but it often
rhymes."
Sir John Templeton

"Everyone has a plan. Too many people use
the 'wing-it-strategy."

"Planning is simply looking into the future to make that future as predictable as you possible can."

"Planning is like a jig saw puzzle. Once you assemble all the pieces together a beautiful picture is created."

"A retirement plan is simply having the picture on the box."
(just like in a jig saw puzzle)
Jim Yih

"People often complain about lack of time when the lack of direction is the real problem."
Zig Ziglar

"If you don't know where you are going, how can you expect to get there?"

"Good plans shape good decisions. That's why good planning helps to make elusive dreams come true."

"Have a plan. Follow the plan, and you'll be surprised how successful you can be. Most people simply don't have a plan."

"If you don't design your own life plan, chances are you'll fall into someone else's plan. And guess what they have planned for you? Not much."

"An economist is an expert who will know tomorrow why the things he predicted yesterday didn't happen."

"Planning is bringing the future into the present so that you can do something about it now."

"A good plan is like a road map: it shows the final destination and usually the best way to get there."

"With every destination, there are many different ways to get there. The best way is the one that suits you best."

"The best plan is simply a sequence of actions towards an objective."

"He who fails to plan, plans to fail"
Ancient proverb

"A good plan today is better than a perfect plan tomorrow."

"Either you run your life or your life runs you. Figure out who's in control."

"People spend more time planning 15 day vacations than they do 15 years of retirement."

"No matter who you are, it's never too late to plan. The best time to start is now. Sooner is better."

"Half the battle is making sure you are on the right road. The other half is how you pay attention to that road."

"My interest is in the future because I am going to spend the rest of my life there."
Charles Kettering

"If you don't know where you are going, you are bound to be somewhere else."
Yogi Berra

notes

notes

notes

Quotes on
TAX

Tax is one of those things that most people don't want to talk about despite the fact that it is one of two certainties in life. The other is death.

Despite the fact that taxes can be complex and terribly misunderstood, it's such an important aspect of personal finance and wealth accumulation.

Tax planning is far more important than investment planning because it can make a bigger difference to the bottom line. Good investment planning can increase returns by 1%, 2%, 3%, 4% or 5%. Good tax planning can improve returns by 10%, 20%, 30%, 40% or 50%. Which planning will give you a better return?

"The hardest thing to understand is income tax."
Albert Einstein

"People who complain about taxes fall into two categories - men and women."
Barry Steiner

"Anyone who believes that Canada's only two official languages are English and French has never read the Income Tax Act."
Marc Denhez

"Taxation is the gentle art of picking feathers off the goose in such a way as to get the greatest amount of feathers with the least amount of squawking."

"It's not about how much you make that counts, it's how much you keep that makes all the difference."

"Understanding tax is the foundation of all financial decisions."

"Tax planning is far more important than tax preparation."

"It is human nature to feel the pain of loss twice as much as the joy of gain."

notes

notes

Quotes on
Learning

As someone who teaches people in workshops, I love the fact that I can help others learn. What I love most about teaching is that every time I do it, I also become the student. Learning is so cool. I learn something new every single day.

What's even cooler is watching my kids learn. They are like little sponges and they don't even realize how proud I am when I see how and what they are learning.

Having kids not only reminds me about the importance of learning but also the importance of experiencing. When kids learn, they are so innocent. They don't see the barrier to learning like adults see.

Is it possible that we let too many hurdles or obstacles get in the way of our learning?

We as adults need to embrace learning. We need to look past the obstacles of learning. No matter how old or young we are, we will become better with knowledge and education.

"Give a man a fish and he eats for a day. Teach a man how to fish and he eats for a lifetime."

"A man's mind, once stretched by new idea, never regains its original dimensions."
Oliver Wendell Holmes

"Learning is a treasure that will follow its owner everywhere."
Chinese Proverb

"Learn as much as you can while you are young (no matter how old you are) because life becomes too busy later on."

"Learning is a lifetime process, but there comes a time when we must stop adding and simply start updating."
Robert Brault

"Anyone who stops learning is old, whether at twenty or eighty."
Henry Ford

"An investment in knowledge pays the best interest."
Benjamin Franklin

"The best gift you can give a student is curiosity because curiosity creates a lifetime of learning."

"Learn from yesterday,
Live for today and
Hope for tomorrow."
Albert Einstein

"We learn more by looking for the answer to a question and not finding it that we do from finding the answer itself."

"You will learn more from doing and failing than not doing anything at all."

"Live as it you were going to die tomorrow. Learn as if you were going to live forever."
Ghandi

"I cannot teach anybody anything. I can only make them think."
Socrates

"The only real mistake is the one in which we learn nothing."

"Retention is the best when the learner is involved."

"The biggest enemy to learning is the teacher who talks too much."

notes

notes

notes

QUOTES
On Love

As a left-brain thinker, love is not always an easy concept to get. I've always believed that destiny is created by every choice and action that you make. I truly believe in the power of the mind and when you want something bad enough you can get it. This mental belief has served me well.

Love is not like this. You can love someone all you want but they may not love you back. Love is two way. It's one of those foo-foo things that's intangible. It's one of those things you can't touch but you can feel.

Love is one of those things where you don't know you have it until you have it. Liz has made me a believer in love and destiny. Not everything can or needs to be controlled.

Now that I have a taste of it, love is more important than anything. What is success, wealth and happiness if you do not have someone to share it with? This is one aspect in my life, where I am truly lucky to have someone to love and someone that loves me.

"True love stories never have endings."

A bell is no bell 'til you ring it,
A song is no song 'til you sing it,
And love in your heart
Wasn't put there to stay -
Love isn't love
'Til you give it away.
Sound of Music

"Children need your presence more than
your presents."
Jesse Jackson

"Sometimes the shortest distance between
two points is a winding path walked arm in
arm. "
Robert Brault

"Will you love me in December
as you do in May,
Will you love me in the good
old fashioned way?
When my hair has all turned gray,
Will you kiss me then and say,
That you love me in December
as you do in May?"
James J. Walker

"Anything in moderation is good
... Except love"

"You are my sunshine, my only sunshine
You make me happy when skies are grey
And don't you know boy,
how much I love you?
Please don't take my sunshine away."

"Destiny is something I had a tough time
believing in until I found true love."

"We waste time looking for the perfect lover,
instead of creating the perfect love."
Tom Robbins

"One of the greatest things you can hear is
when someone says 'I Love You'"

"To love is nothing
To be loved is something
To love and be loved is everything."

"Love is the malfunction of the heart
Which weakens the brain,
Causes eyes to sparkle
Cheeks to glow,
Blood pressure to rise,
And lips to pucker."

"Love puts the fun in together, the sad in apart, and the joy in a heart."

"To love someone deeply gives you strength
Being loved by someone gives you courage."
Lao Tzu

"When the power of love overcomes the love of power, the world will know peace."
Jimi Hendrix

"Love is work: the more you give, the more you get back."

"There is no special formula to love:
You learn to love by taking risks
You learn to love by loving."

"The smile on your face let's me know that
you need me.
The truth in your eyes saying you'll never
leave me.
The touch of your hand says you'll catch me
wherever I fall.
"You say it best when you say nothing at all."
Allison Krause

notes

notes

notes

Other favorite
QUOTES

"Everything in your life gets better when you get better, and nothing is ever going to get better until you get better."
Larry Winget

"Be authentic. Don't try to be someone you aren't. You'll hate yourself for it and the effort to maintain the facade will exhaust you. BE REAL! Many won't like the real you but that's better than having people adore the person that isn't you at all."
Larry Winget

"Clean up your own backyard. Change by example. Just be the way you want others to be and hope they pay attention."
Larry Winget

"Discipline is the bridge between goals and accomplishment."

"Don't just read the easy stuff. You may be entertained by it, but you will never grow from it."

"Formal education will make you a living; self-education will make you a fortune."

"Happiness is not something you postpone for the future; it is something you design for the present. "

"Time is more valuable than money. You can get more money, but you cannot get more time."
Jim Rohn

"The problem with common sense is it's just not common enough"

"Wealth is simple, not easy
Health is simple, not easy
Life is simple, not easy"

"Jim, if you want to lose weight you have to
do 2 simple things: Eat less and exercise
more. As you always say . . . it's simple, just
not easy."
Liz Yih

"Most of the fundamental ideas of science
are essentially simple, and may, as a rule, be
expressed in a language comprehensible to
everyone."
Albert Einstein

"The main purpose of science is simplicity
and as we understand more things,
everything should become simpler."

"Reward comes in reaching your destination. Satisfaction comes from the journey."

"Sometimes the EASY way is far from the RIGHT way."

"Don't just teach your kids to be happy. Teach them the difference between right and wrong."

"One reason so few of us achieve what we truly want is that we never direct our focus; we never concentrate our power. Most people dabble their way through life, never deciding to master anything in particular."
Tony Robbins

"Focus 90% of your time on solutions and only 10% of your time on problems."

"There's something to be said about the KISS principle: Keep It Simple Stupid."

"Focus your energy on things you can control because worrying about things you can't control wastes too much precious energy."

"Most people are comfortable. That's the problem. People never make changes when they are comfortable."

"People are an important part of your past, present, and future. The best thing for your future is to hang around people you want to be."

"Everyday you live, you are living your legacy. Stay focused on what is important and live life forward!"

"Before you ask more from others, ask more from yourself first."

"When you were born, you cried and everybody else was happy. The only question that matters is this - when you die, will you be happy when everybody else is crying?"
Tony Campolo

"Everything we accomplish in life, we accomplish with the help of others so surround yourself with the right people and you can't help but accomplish a lot."

"If you have much, give of your wealth; If you have little, give of your heart."

"You get the best out of others when you give the best of yourself."

"Everyone has something to give:
Some people give time, some money, some
their skills and connections, some literally
give their life's blood."

"We can never obtain peace in the outer
world until we make peace with ourselves."
Dalai Lama

"Knowing is not enough, you must apply
Willing is not enough, you must do."
Goethe

"The definition of insanity is doing the same
thing over and over again and expecting
different results."
Albert Einstein

"The secret to future success is to create a
predictable future."

"Energy is the elixir of life.
Passion + health + humor + people = energy"
Loretta Laroche

"People don't care how much you know until
they know how much you care."

"Life can only be understood backwards.
Unfortunately, it must be lived forward."
Soren Kierkegaard

"Change is the law of life. Those who look
only to the past or present are certain to miss
the future."
John F Kennedy

"Nothing Great in this world has been
accomplished without passion."
Oprah Winfrey

"You are not paid to work hard. In fact, you are not paid for effort at all. You are paid for results. It's not what you do; it's what you get done."
Larry Winget

"It takes twice as much effort of focus on the negative as it does to focus on the positive. Conserve your energy."

"Do not leave the education of your kids solely in the hands of teachers. Parents have a responsibility to be accountable for the education of their children.

"Let no one ever come to you without leaving better and happier."
Mother Theresa

"I will not let anyone walk through my mind
with their dirty feet."
Ghandi

"Your choices today allow you to leave your
affairs at the end of your life as a lasting
legacy. Either you will be remembered for
how well you lived life or you will be
remembered for the big mess you left behind
for others to clean up."

"The key to a great life is shifting your focus
from accumulation to contribution."
Robin Sharma

"DANCE like no one is watching,
LOVE like you've never been hurt,
SING like no one can hear you,
LIVE as though heaven is on earth."

notes

notes

notes

notes

About Jim

Google Jim Yih and you will see that he has extensive media coverage and significant web presence. As a professional financial speaker, best selling author, syndicated columnist and financial expert, Jim is passionate about financial education and helping people make better decisions with money. Jim's 20 years of experience in the financial industry helps people demystify investing, retirement, and personal finance. His passion to educate is seen in his relentless development of financial education tools, resources and products including audio CDs and software programs.

Financial Speaker

Jim is one of Canada's leading experts on money, retirement, investing and personal finance. He has a passion for teaching and helping people make better decisions with money so they can all retire happy and achieve financial wellness.

As a well-known financial speaker, he has entertained audiences large and small with his common sense 'to the point' approach. Audiences rave about Jim's ability to take complex matters and deliver them in a way that makes sense.

Jim has entertained, educated and inspired audiences all across the country. In every presentation, his goal is simple: To say something that makes people better, smarter, happier and wealthier. He believes that education can only exist if there is a connection between himself and his audience. He is passionate about combining stories, humor, creativity and inspiring messages to create the connection.

He believes that true success of a professional speaker comes from not only education but also entertainment and inspiration. His use of humor and real life stories make Jim's presentations memorable and delightful. Jim is the consummate professional who strives to make a difference in the lives of the people he touches. His goal in every presentation is to share light bulb moments so his audience can achieve more success, wealth and happiness.

To hire Jim for your next function visit www.JimYih.com.

Financial Education

Jim is the founder and CEO of his company The Think Box. Think Box specializes in putting financial education programs in the workplace.

Think Box caters to employers who care about the financial well being of their employees. We are the perfect complement to both existing wellness programs, as will as Group Retirement Programs like pensions and Group RRSP programs. We take ordinary Group Retirement Plans and turn them into exceptional ones by providing fun, engaging and unique education programs.

We simply take employee education and service to a new level. We help employers and their businesses by delivering financial education programs that employees rave about.

For more information, visit www.ThinkBoxHome.com.

Good Research leads to Good Decisions

Education and knowledge are the roots of financial success. Beyond Jim's articles, presentations and individual consulting, Jim has developed a suite of products to help people achieve more success, wealth and happiness.

To learn more about Jim's books, CDs, videos and software programs, visit his website www.JimYih.com

Retire Happy Blog

For the past 20 years, Jim's professional passion has been helping people to retire happy and make retirement the best years the best years.

In addition to his speaking and his time working with individual clients, Jim has spent the last 15 years writing articles.   Google Jim and you will see his articles have hit many mainstream media sources like the Edmonton Journal, National Post, Globe and Mail, Moneysense, Yahoo.ca, Canadian Business, Fundlibrary and many more.

All of Jim's articles can be found on his website www.RetireHappyBlog.ca. Check it out as it can be an incredible learning resource.

Made in the USA
Charleston, SC
08 September 2014